The Night Blooming Jasmine in Your Heart

The Night Blooming Jasmine in Your Heart

MARIE HELENA

Mystic Marks

Dawn Light Press

USA

Dawn Light Press

an imprint of
Lillicat Publishers
9625 Mission Gorge Road, B2-159
Santee, California, 92071
USA

Cover design Copyright 2017 by Victor Habbick Visions. Vhabbick@mac.com
www.victorhabbick.com
Special thanks to Susan Menanno for her permission to use her words and ideas in
"A Secret Energy Source." Copyright 2017 by Susan Menanno.
www.ShamanWalks.org

Gift Edition
First Print Edition: June 2017
Printed and Bound in USA

Print ISBN: 978-1-945646-22-5
EPUB ISBN: 978-1-945646-23-2
MOBI ISBN: 978-1-945646-24-9

For my precious, loving family . . .

The gift of my journey.

*Life is the flower for which
love is the honey.*

~ Victor Hugo

Table of Contents

Foreword

I *will never forget the day that I met Marie Helena Pokora.*

Marie had been busy at work designing spiritual bookmarks she called ***Mystic Marks: Bookmarks for the Soul***. She had found me online and fallen in love with the poetry of my company sobriquet: *She Who Weaves the Web*. Determined to make a connection, she had contacted me to talk about the creation of a website for her bookmarks.

She came to our appointment that day and we clicked right away. I loved Marie and her beautiful energy, I loved her bookmarks, but mostly what I loved was Marie's writing . . . her way with words . . . her attention to the way that words lay into the senses of the soul! In every sense of the word, I realized that I was sitting in the presence of a true wordsmith and a very wise woman. Even in the inspirational sayings she crafted for her bookmarks, I could see that this woman was a writer and would one day need a much bigger canvas than a bookmark!

We had made such a wonderful connection during our session and I felt like Marie was committed to coming out with her bookmarks. So I was thrilled when she called me back and said that she wanted to work with me to create her website, but that it would be some time before she would be ready. So I filed her plan away and kind of just forgot about it. Nearly two years later, when Marie called announcing "I'm ready to do it!" it was like no time had passed. I was deeply impressed by her perseverance. Later, I would discover that staying true is Marie's hallmark.

The journey of developing Marie's website was an exciting, magical co-creation and we really got to know each other on a whole new level. When I had first met Marie, she was one of my first clients after changing the focus of my web design company from *BizTech* to *Weaves the Web*. The renaming of my company signified a big spiritual shift for me as I was moving into predominantly serving people who were raising their own consciousness to help other people through humanitarian, spiritual, creative, and healing means. Marie certainly fit the bill! And, in fact, Marie not only became my star client, she became my star friend.

With that kind of writing talent there was no way that I was going to let Marie get away without having a blog on her website. It was a part of my general process as a web designer to let my clients know about how important blogging can be as a way to help your audience get to know you. This was years before social media was prevalent. At that time, it was becoming obvious that the internet was a great forum for anyone to become "published." So what better way to prime the well and get started writing than through blogging? But, alas, many of my clients simply would or could not do it. So when Marie started cranking out the blog articles slowly at first and then more regularly, I would use her as an example to show my other clients how it's done. But the truth is Marie had something special. She not only had a great gift for writing, she also had the great gift of perseverance. And she had a unique voice. Through all the ups and downs of her life, year after year, Marie continued to write. And the blogs became her passion, the JOY of her life, the record of her journey and what she had been learning.

As is the way of all true earth angels and messengers of the soul, it always seemed like Marie's choice of topics was just what you needed that day. Her ability to track life events through synchronicity, relationships, and personal responsibility makes her writing powerful and what she has to say relevant and potent. As we read along through Marie's storytelling and life weavings, we get a sense of someone who has been there and done that and has come through to the other side into a land of day. She has this beautiful way of making sense out of things in life that are difficult or challenging and sharing it in words and stories that are inspiring, pertinent, and poignant.

There is something more I'd like you to know about Marie. Speaking of Marie's steadfastness, every year for the last seven years, Marie Helena Pokora has sent me a Christmas gift and a birthday gift. It's as though she is an angel to the angels, having made some kind of promise before we were born to bless, inspire, and uplift me in this way. Sometimes, that gift has been a very bright spot in a very dark time. Even though she is unfailing in this deed, I am always taken by surprise and delighted when the package comes and I realize who it is from. Each time the gift itself is full of synchronicity, giving me confirmation of something in my life that Marie would have no way of knowing about. What a joy this is!

One might think that with this kind of devotion that Marie is a relative or a sister, but I've only met Marie in the physical once. You just know when you meet a kindred spirit and are connected soul to soul. In my tradition we say, "All is my relation." Marie has made that come alive for me in a way that is very real and life affirming. She has shown me the power of soul sisters! Marie and I don't talk all the time or even stay in touch in the physical, but we are never far apart and the soul connection we have deeply inspires and lifts my life.

Marie Helena Pokora had a dream and she followed her bliss. She never gave up and in that we witness how the journey becomes the destination. It is so gratifying to know that Marie's writings will lift the lives of even more people so that others can connect to her in this way as Marie now shares her words and wisdom with us all through her new book, *The Night Blooming Jasmine in Your Heart*. May all the hands that hold this book and the eyes that see the pages and read the messages be blessed by these words!

Thank you, Marie, for bringing forth your book, *The Night Blooming Jasmine in Your Heart*. YOU are the true gift. You are a true messenger and even knowing that someone like you exists on this earth and that you can now touch even more lives as you have touched mine is grace. You are a jewel in the crown of humanity.

~Rev. Renee Bledsoe

Preface

I love Irving Berlin's song *"There's No Business Like Show Business"* and my greatest joy has recently become waking up in the morning and waiting for the *SHOW* to begin. Several years of spiritual searching have taught me that the *Divine Universe* can't wait to bring forth a parade of amazing *SYNCHRONICITIES*–beautiful messages supporting the hopes and dreams of my *Higher Self*. Reflecting my intention and energy . . . Inspiring me to make new connections . . . Revealing me to myself . . . Showing me the beauty that surrounds me . . . Encouraging me to speak my truth . . . Encouraging me to bless *EVERYTHING* . . . and Teaching me how to change the *STORY* of my life. As Neale Donald Walsch would phrase it, guiding me to the *"next, grandest version of myself."*

On my way to this discovery, I experienced a number of physical issues (messages) which served to convince me to release the fear response of endless attempts to find solutions to every problem and gratefully *SURRENDER* to *Divine Guidance* as my *Source of Light and Love*. And to understand that all lessons are gifts. Every experience is meant to teach us something. Once we grasp the lesson, we come closer to knowing our true selves. When the intellect connects with the heart and we learn to listen to and honor our bodies and the still, small voice inside us, we can find the lesson in *EVERYTHING*. We know that we are gifted with all that is necessary to accomplish this.

The *Mystic Marks* book series begins with *The Night Blooming Jasmine in Your Heart*.

This series is the legacy of my life journey. The search to find my dharma . . . to find what I love to do . . . what brings me into flow . . . and to share with others what has brought me peace.

Marie Helena

Acknowledgments

*I*n Celebration of the *LOVE* that dances so beautifully through my life!

My deepest GRATITUDE and APPRECIATION to:

Archangels Michael, *my protector . . .* ***Gabriel***, *my co-creator . . .* ***Haniel,*** *my guiding spirit;*

My parents, ***Richard and Agatha,*** *who encouraged and supported me so beautifully every time I wanted to learn something new;*

My wonderful sister ***Shirley***, *our family angel, with whom I began and continue my spiritual exploration;*

My brother ***Gerry*** *whose delightful (and often surprising) wit keeps me grounded;*

My husband ***Dan*** *who lovingly critiques my writing and channels spiritual messages for me;*

*My daughter **Valerie** for her irresistible joy and creativity in the publishing and marketing of my work;*

*My daughter **Rachel** for her loving support and professional counsel and guidance in the publishing of this book;*

*My son-in-law **Jim** for his generous and unconditional assistance and open heart;*

*My son-in-law **Kevin** for the gift of his new presence in our family;*

*My grandsons **Colin** and **Dylan** for their enthusiastic interest and support and beautiful hearts;*

*My sister-in-law **Robbie** from whom love streams so joyously;*

*My brother-in-law **Ted** for his profound generosity;*

*My brother-in-law **Joe**, fellow artist, for his continuing interest and encouragement;*

*My devoted nieces **Cindy, Laura and Julie** for their celebration of my work;*

***Georgiann Voissem** who introduced me to LifeLine and changed the way I live;*

***Renee Bledsoe** who designed my website with unparalleled beauty and sensitivity;*

***Ken Porter,** Hakomi Therapist, my muse;*

***Abraham Hicks** who helps me remember Who I Truly Am;*

***TJ Sally** who magically appeared from the mists to celebrate* *my writing;*

Carrol Fix *who fell in love with my blogs and offered to publish them;*

Julia Altamar *and* **Pamela Hope DeLuca**, *my soul sisters and* **Roby Azzah**, *my soul brother;*

Kwai Chee Low, *Medical Qigong Practitioner, who sent me his healing energy from Kuala Lumpur;*

Candy Norder, *my dear friend, who travels every journey with me;*

Matt Jones *and* **Darren Burmania** *for their compassionate legal guidance;*

The many doctors who read my blogs with delight and appreciation: **Dr. Kenneth Dudley, Dr. Allyn Peelen, Dr. Jerry Mulder, Jr., Dr. Daniel VanGessel, Dr. Rod Taber;**

and, finally,

Dr. Bruce Vankerschaver, *who envisioned the title* **Mystic Marks** *before I had written my first blog.*

Special Acknowledgment to **Susan Mennano**
(A Secret Energy Source)
Susan has been practicing Shamanism for decades. Her goal is to empower people to be true to who they are. She guides Spirit Quests and Journey' as well as doing Shamanic Soul Readings, Chakra Clearing and Cleansing, and Soul Retrievals. You can contact her at www.ShamanWalks.org.

© lamnee

Introduction

On a dark, moonlit night most of nature's floral offerings excuse themselves from the diligence of the day and nod off to silent slumber, releasing their daytime rigors and replenishing their energies in anticipation of the first break of dawn. But there are several verdant beauties that choose to blossom instead in the velvety night, stirring under the exquisite luminescence of Mother Moon.

The **Night Blooming Jasmine** is one of these nocturnal angels. And, it seems, in choosing the blackness of the evening boulevard, it displays to us a special wisdom in this enterprise.

It does not engage with the clamor and bustle of the day but rather awaits the peace and tranquility of the eventide and, in this gentle ambiance, it quietly attunes itself to the senses and sounds surrounding it . . .

the whisper of the wind,
the hooting owl,
flitting fireflies,
wandering spiders.

It feels the majesty of the moon sailing in the sky, intuitively embracing the knowledge and wisdom crossing its path, rather than attempting to dispense counsel itself.

The beautiful **Night Blooming Jasmine** is an exquisite offering. It embraces Nature's gifts with a full and open heart and is so bountiful with its grace that it can perfume the air with a heavenly scent even in the bright light of noon time with its blooms resting softly closed.

As always, Nature continues to gift us with metaphors of a life well-lived.

Is there a **Night Blooming Jasmine** or other flower in your heart waiting to guide you to the beauty and knowledge and wisdom that you have been too busy to see . . . or inspire you to infuse the moments of life with your personal, loving soul signature?

Please wander with me through the musings of my heart as I share the words that effortlessly flow from the profound vibrations of the Divine and loving Universe.

© JuliaBadeeva

Make Something Beautiful...

There are many profound philosophers in the world
. . . thinkers of great thoughts, deep introspection,
challenging suppositions . . . sharing their answers to life's
great questions: *Why are we here? How should we navigate
this earthly journey? What is truly significant?*

Many of these brilliant individuals have lived before us;
some are with us now all leaving us the treasure of their
experience through their magnificent words, their art, their
music. Often, we are inspired by the messages of these gifts
and, if they feel resonant to us, we choose to embrace what
feels in concert with our souls.

*The lessons we learn instruct and guide us as we navigate
our daily lives, which are often replete with challenges
and invitations to become more than we presently are.* The
lessons often give us careful steps to follow regarding how
to acknowledge, accept, embrace, experience and release
the issues that are plaguing us . . . issues that may have
followed us throughout our lives, painful remnants of days

gone by, problems left unsolved and unsettled.

The serendipitous messages that flow from these artists and philosophers guide us through moments of chaos and cacophony, helping us come to resolution of difficult and embroiled issues. This is a worthy goal. A true achievement.

As I formulate my own philosophy of guiding principles for my life and embrace the perceptions of the philosophers which sing to my soul, *I feel a longing to do more* . . . to take a step beyond achieving the "settling" of the issue at hand.

I have come to imagine the delight of taking the resolution of a problem and Making Something Beautiful out of each puzzling Gordian knot, leaving my *"Signature"* in that moment as an artist would portray his original conception, embossing and inscribing each challenge with evidence of *Love* and *Beauty*. I aspire to transcending their boundaries, infusing them with a luminous outpouring of grace, imprinting each challenge which enters my life with beauty and light and the glorious vibration of dazzling, radiant love.

This kind of endeavor is a completely personal one as each of our lives carries its own stories and stumbling blocks. Like the artist, it is we who can choose to *Make Something Beautiful* out of the raw material of our lives.

This is a supremely creative act and a deeply satisfying one. It is immensely empowering for no matter what enters our lives, we have a canvas waiting for us to find the *"Beautiful"* as we uniquely envision it, solving an issue of great discord with an open heart and a beautiful grace that engages and animates our souls.

© anamad

Morning Prayer

*T*oday I will become
The Next, Grandest Version of Myself.

*Just as a sapphire pond smiles gratefully at the sun's embrace,
I will flow my energy to every person I encounter, warming
their day with my curiosity and caring.*

*Just as the wind weaves its spell amidst the flora of the forest,
I will weave my wonder at this glorious body I inhabit.*

*Just as the night covers the earth with its blanket of protection,
I will still my efforts to complete the mighty list I have
imagined for myself. I will honor my weariness and comfort
myself with peace.*

*Just as the stars glisten in the evening sky,
my soul will shimmer with gratitude for the bouquet of gifts
that have found their way into my heart.*

*I will watch the earth for its whispers of guidance
and let it lead me into my grace-filled day.*

Setting the Angel Free

W*e have all experienced very special moments in our lives* when the things we say and do are beautiful, inspired, affirming, and encouraging to others. Everything flows unerringly from our intuition . . . our sense of knowing . . . about what is important in life. These are sacred shimmerings of grace when we affect others in a profound way with our love, caring, and compassion.

THIS is Who We Truly Are.

But there are also moments when we say and do things that are not filled with love and generosity, when our pride or ego or fear orchestrates our thoughts, words, and actions and negative emotions spill out of us like emotionally orphaned children who have not been loved and shown how wonderful they are.

And, like those orphaned children, in this space we do not reside fully in the safe and powerful place of knowing our true worth. And so we are left with a broken image which we try to repair at times by pointing out to others what is wrong with them, thereby attempting to prove to ourselves that we are right.

We feel lost in the illusion that we are not OK.

But this behavior of ours which naturally produces discomfort and unrest is ONLY indicative of the trappings of earth school. This is not who we are. It proceeds from the role of LIMITATION, which we willingly embraced in this dimension in order to learn how to transcend it, expanding the spiritual evolution of ourselves and all earth dwellers.

We have the ability to go forth, learn to witness and reflect upon our choices and actions and change what does not bring us peace and soul satisfaction.

We can learn to listen to our hearts for guidance and direction regarding our choice of how to live.

We can turn away from the efforts of our egos to prevail—our attempts to prove our worthiness—and recognize, instead, that we are all journeying together, learning to find what makes us truly happy.

*And it is in that **transcension**, that stunning return to our spiritual heritage, when all of our actions are sourced in **LOVE**, that only joy and happiness flow through us. **THIS** is the glory of Who We Truly Are*, the touchstone of the transcendent return to our spiritual field of dreams.

*I saw the angel in the marble and carved until
I set him free.*

~Michelangelo

© natikka

The Eyes and Ears of Love

*I*t's a gray, gloomy day and you have just dragged your weary body out of bed. Sighing, you reflect on what is waiting for your attention. What happens next depends on the *CHOICE* you make about how to experience your day.

You can predict and expect a difficult scenario with a long to-do list of things you DO NOT want to do . . . or . . .

You can be the eyes and ears of Love, just looking for beautiful things to enjoy.

Like the shower-rain cascading down your body, waking up your sleepy skin with a splash of good morning messages leaving you refreshed and now wide-awake and alert . . .
Like the bounce of your sneakers and the comfort and warmth of your snuggly socks . . . Like the allure of coffee brightly brewing just for your pleasure . . . And the bed you just made with pillows fluffed and blankets smoothed, ready for your next sojourn that evening . . . And the scent of the freshly mowed grass of your early bird neighbor . . . And the stirrings of other family members beginning their preparations for the day.

Gray day or not . . . you have just started **YOUR day** *with an abundant supply of beautiful inner weather because you* **CHOSE** *to look for things to appreciate. Beauty is in the eye of the beholder. And you, beautiful soul that you are, know that the* **Divine Universe** *loves you unconditionally and has gifted you with many simple pleasures and, therefore, you are eager to uncover, discover, and revel in their glory.*

You are finding everything right and beautiful and joyous in the world. And that's your **spectacular** *life!*

© Karma

Irish Taxi Drivers

"*Hello, luv . . . good morning to you . . . and are you here on holiday?*" This is the beautiful way I was greeted nearly every time I stepped into a taxi in Galway, Ireland.

I have just returned from a trip abroad to visit my daughter Rachel on sabbatical there and I truly must say that the taxi drivers in Ireland so warmed my heart. I was able to sit up front with them in what we would call the driver's seat here in the U.S., as the steering wheels there are placed on the right side of the car, and so I got the wonderful opportunity to ask a few questions and learn so much about their lives.

I heard about pride in their families, about their wives and children (names, ages, and personalities), about how the college-age kids were driving them to the "poor house" and how they had learned to step out of the fray and, thankfully, let their brilliant wives negotiate with their teen-age daughters. I heard about last night's christening celebration that threatened to turn into a brawl until the taxi driver stepped in and told the offending party to get his priorities straightened out. I heard many comments about the recession and how it had dampened somewhat the spirits of the Irish. (I can hardly imagine what they were like before!) And, when I mentioned that I was visiting my daughter but leaving soon, I heard the comment, "Not to worry for we'll be keeping an eye on her."

The sense of living life in the Present Moment and embracing it with such passion are so strong in Ireland it is truly amazing. If I had known what I could find there in the open hearts of the Irish, I would have gotten myself to the Emerald Isle long before this.

Whenever I left the taxi, I always commented to the driver my wish that he have a beautiful day. And I always received a beautiful smile and blessing in return. Irish eyes sparkle with fun and mischief and delight in what the day will bring. What a lovely inspiration! ***I am now determined to find the "Irish" in everyone I encounter*** *and am set on uncovering this beautiful gift embedded in every human heart!*

© pronoia

Fatima's Laughter

***I** have this lovely group of friends . . . individuals that I used to work with . . . who like to get together a few times a year to celebrate our birthdays.* It's always a convivial affair. We catch up with everyone's latest escapades and adventures. There is much merriment and lots of affectionate teasing (especially by the guys) which are enjoyed by all. And, amid this friendly chatter, there is always one particular moment I so look forward to . . . the delight of *"hearing" one of my special friends arrive* . . . and that is because *I can recognize her glorious bursts of laughter* before she even enters the room.

*Truly, my friend **Fatima** cannot contain her **JOY**. It pours out of her like liquid grace SPARKLING with tiny diamonds of delight.* And I am filled with gratitude to catch *the happy sparks* as they flutter by. *Our delightful Fatima is completely taken with life . . . so present, so interested in what is going on around her. And not only interested, but CELEBRATORY!*

When I hear her laughter in the offing, I cannot wait for Fatima to arrive. It is so lovely and engaging to be around someone so radiantly interested in and appreciative of everything she encounters. I think she must have been one of the first in the heavenly line to receive Curiosity and then must have promptly snuck eagerly into the aisles of ***Joyfulness*** and ***Delight***. I am not sure why I have the good fortune to know this memorable character who graces my life. But I do recognize her spirit as a special ***GIFT.*** She is a reminder to me of the ***charismatic connection*** we can all enjoy with everything that crosses our path.

There is ALWAYS something beautiful to behold, to be fascinated with and to enjoy just by reason of its very existence, its availability.

We live on a verdant, lush planet of infinite possibility. We are surrounded by fascinating individuals, each with his or her own preferences, experiences, values, feelings. Everyone has a story to tell.

Fatima is listening. And seeing. And appreciating. She is present. And, best of all, she is ENJOYING the ride. Fatima will not miss "the party." Not with that glorious curiosity and boundless appreciation. *She IS "the party!"*
Have you discovered YOUR invitation to this glorious event?

© natalia9

Breakthrough!

*H*ere's a steppingstone that will move us forward when we feel locked in a place of negative emotion.

We know what we feel in a given situation and we don't like it. But it's difficult to move past it. At the same time, we can clearly see where we would like to be and it's a *Higher Self* position. But we are *not there yet*.

Perhaps, at this critical moment, we can take a breath, center ourselves, and make this simple statement, using **whatever words** fit the moment.

This is what I aspire to:

I aspire to be loving and compassionate.
I aspire to forgive the hurt.
I aspire to see where my ego is entering into this situation.
I aspire to be centered and peaceful.
I aspire to take beautiful care of myself.
I aspire to speak my truth.
I aspire to listen to yours.

Just the mere utterance to ourselves and to others of these powerful words: ***This is what I aspire to*** will be a personal and public declaration of where we intend to go with our reaction and what we intend to do about it. We are giving notice to the lower vibrations circling around us that they are on their way out of this picture. We have declared our intention to let the ***SUNSHINE*** in and act from a foundation of ***LOVE***.

This beautiful message helps us relieve our suffering and also assists others to see what we are intending to accomplish. There is a softening that occurs when these words are uttered, in our hearts and in the hearts of those around us.

I have never seen these words fail to make a difference. They're a form of alchemy . . . making gold out of base metal.

One step forward . . . *but a very important one* . . . ***in bringing in the Light!***

© la_balaur

Listen for the Feelings

Society often considers multi-tasking to be a noteworthy accomplishment.

"Look at all the things she can do," we exclaim admiringly at an individual who has perfected this skill and wonder how we could ever juggle that list of must-do items in one day.

No, for some of us, things take longer. Perhaps we pay very close attention to where we are. And it isn't just our tasks and chores that totally engage us. Conversations, in particular, often take longer than we might have anticipated. Sometimes, we are looking for just a yes or no answer from someone to one of our questions but those simple words may have a bevy of emotions attached to them. And concerns and feelings which initially seem simple often tumble into new layers of revelation as we turn our full attention to the speaker, offering safety, caring, and compassion.

If you are an individual who is able to take in the "layers" that reveal themselves as a conversation unfolds, kudos to you because you are someone who can LISTEN FOR THE

FEELINGS. Someone who can appreciate the authenticity coming your way. Someone who can be totally present . . . without expectation . . . and open to whatever is presenting itself in that moment. And, yes, it is not the skill of multi-tasking, but it is much, much more.

It is "holding space" for the human heart. Being patiently there while the "message" finds its way to self-expression. It is a beautiful gift of self . . . a gift of love . . . ***PRESENCE.***

When we choose to step up and ***"listen for the feelings"*** when someone engages our attention, it will, undoubtedly, be an investment of our time and energy. But the reward is an even closer connection to the individual with whom we are interacting and an amazing opportunity to expand the corridors of our own hearts!

© Tatiana Ka

Ichabod's Night Life

It was a windy night in Galway, Ireland. I was visiting my daughter Rachel who is on sabbatical there and I was sleeping in her guest bedroom. Rachel's apartment house is located on a peninsula on Galway Bay. It sits literally in the middle of the harbor and, if you look outside of her window, you can see sailboats of all sizes lined up and moored to the docks.

On this particular evening, I was awakened by the sound of someone apparently working on a boat in the middle of the night. There was a *persistent clanging* . . . actually two different clangings . . . and it felt like one was agitating the other. My daughter had told me earlier that she slept with earplugs because of the harbor noises, but I didn't feel a little background sound would make a difference to me. I was wrong.

That night I tossed restlessly for hours, growing a strong frustration that intensified every time I heard another sound. I could hardly believe that someone had decided to work on his boat at this hour. The logic was beyond me. I went to the window of the bedroom and parted the curtains. The boats were sitting in the water magically illuminated by the mooring lights. The scene was breathtakingly beautiful . . . and there was no one to be seen working in the area. Confused, I looked further and discovered that the wind was willfully whipping the branches of a very tall tree against the night sky.

So, I thought, it's the wind I have to deal with and decided I would try to use my consciousness to slow it down. (I had read on a couple of occasions that it is possible to move a cloud, so I thought I would try changing the speed of the wind.) I was finally able to slow it down enough so that I could get some sleep but decided I needed a better plan for the next night as I was not yet practiced in the art of cloud/wind transport.

We checked the anticipated wind speed for the coming night and, sure enough, a very windy evening was in the offing. I decided to see what resources I could call up because I did not want to go the ear plugs route.

Remembering a very important lesson I had learned from a book called Courageous Dreaming by Alberto Villoldo, I decided that I had to change my story about the clanging. The first night it had represented a series of constant intrusions into my night of peaceful sleep. Now, I decided to call up my imagination and create a new story. In this scenario, the clanging was coming from a phantom sailor called Ichabod. I was asleep on the lower deck of a boat with several sailors. Every night the phantom Ichabod made an appearance on the top deck and proceeded to adjust the masts and moorings, clanging away as he worked. Everyone on the boat knew Ichabod and held a great affection for him. Ichabod's appearance each evening signaled that all was right with the world and, with the clanging reminder of his presence, everyone slept soundly. Including me.

The next morning, I ecstatically celebrated the beautiful way I had been able to "dream" myself into a peaceful place.

Telling myself a new story has become for me a new way to deal with the challenges that present themselves in my life. And it's not always easy. And sometimes I forget to do it. But, oh, when I can remember this lesson and make it happen, I am overjoyed with the knowledge that I can change the way I perceive my reality. I was over the moon about Ichabod. Rachel, too. She has even adopted him as a guest in her harbor home.

In imagining this story, I followed Villoldo's advice to create my story (or dream) by flying to the level of ***eagle*** which is ***spiritually based***. I framed the sound as a peaceful resonance and that is what it became.

If you have a story in your life that is bringing you suffering, I invite and encourage you to call on your power to paint a picture that will soothe and comfort you, delighting your soul and bringing you the peace of Ichabod.

© Egle

The Very Special Grace of the Tulip

During the spring and summer months of the year I love to keep a tall, clear glass vase of beautiful cut flowers on the counter in the kitchen.

I pass by them frequently and they never fail to bring me joy. There is, however, a particular flower that not only reveals to me its color and shape and exquisite design, it also impresses upon my heart the mystery and glory and the wonder of staying-in-the-flow. This lovely flower is the *tulip* and watching it work its magic is almost *mystical*.

The first time I noticed that tulips have this special quality, I was amazed at what I witnessed. Unlike all other flowers, when they are cut and placed in a vase of water, tulips do not stop growing. Their *life force* is so strong that they continue to lengthen and expand and, as they do, they form a lovely arc over the vase.

This beautiful tulip dance reminds me of the *grace of*

surrender (trust in the perfection of the moment), of the beauty of bliss, of the sheer joy of being alive and B R E A T H I N G. Nothing . . . not even the experience of being separated from its root . . . prevents this blossoming forth. You will not see a freshly cut tulip sadly grieving the separation or losing its vitality because circumstances have rearranged its life.

This flower seems the physical incarnation of ***the beauty of a soul*** which trusts and embraces "what is", holds space for it, and continues to radiate wonder.

© Karma

Wings

Our lives are filled with messages waiting to be delivered to us. And the messengers who deliver these revelations are everywhere.

They include everyone we encounter—from our family to our colleagues, sales clerks, repairmen, television personalities, the little boy playing across the street—even the bad-tempered clerk who waited on us in the store, or the driver who cut us off in traffic. **They exist in our world to present to us the life views we hold about ourselves** and they may be engaging and endearing or frustrating and fractious.

If you can summon up some perspective about this and add in a dash of creativity and humor, I have a suggestion regarding how to *enhance and enjoy this experience.* ***Give them all WINGS in your imagination! Make them all angels! They are all actually doing the work of angels* . . .** helping us to see the picture of the world we have created for ourselves and to master the earth work we have undertaken. And, since this is how the earth school system works, we might as well put a big, broad smile on our faces while we learn our lessons.

Consider the visual delight of walking into a GATHERING of family or friends and imagining all of them with their own unique set of wings fluttering in a beat to match their personalities.

The **gregarious individual** would have wide, flapping appendages whisking the air to and fro with the vibration of his excitement.

The **person who loves to sing or hum** would be sporting smooth pinions undulating with a distinctive rhythm.

The **joker** in the group would probably have one of his wings tucked into a piece of clothing so he would attract the second takes he loves so much.

All of these individuals could be illustrating for us the joy and excitement and fun we are experiencing in our lives. In our next encounter, however, we might find **a road rage driver with stress written all over his face.** He, too, would be sporting wings but his accessories might be audacious wings that would move thunderously in a loud, clapping sound.

Now, it may be easy to picture the so-called "nice guys" in the angelic costume but it may seem strange to picture our road rage driver wearing wings and you might wonder how this frustrating individual can fill this angelic role. *Fact is . . . he may be resonating with something inside us,* something unsettled . . . a stress we have not acknowledged, perhaps, or let ourselves experience. And he is showing up in our life to bring this omission to our attention. And here is how he might be an angel to us. **Emotions that are not acknowledged go underground, deep inside us** and often make their next appearance dressed as a major upset, illness, or disease.

So it would behoove us to *welcome ALL of the angels in our life* and give thanks for the messages they bring us regardless of the varying roles they play.

After all, the **Divine Universe** only assigns them the **reflections** of our own mojo so we can "hear" the sounds and "see" the pictures we are making with the way we choose to live our life and learn the lessons we have chosen for our experience here.

So, I say, *WING ON!*

Recognize these DIVINE CREATURES with their dazzling (if imaginary) wings who are educating and enlightening us and enjoy their sometimes affirming, sometimes challenging messages while we earn our own bright and beautiful wings in earth school.

© yoriko katayama

Standing By

*W*hen someone is telling us of his pain or distress, what is the most powerful way we can respond?

First, we truly accept that this experience is a part of the person's **sacred journey** and we **honor** it. We do this by *NOT* presuming to know what is the best thing for this person to do. We trust that this vital and important information is available to *him* *if, as, and when* he chooses to access it. Most importantly, we respond to the emotion he is expressing with the present moment gift of **beautiful, mindful listening and compassion.**

When a person is feeling physical/emotional pain, he responds in a heart-centered way to being comforted and soothed by someone who is truly attempting to understand his feelings. Once a person feels heard and understood and cared about, he is ready to move forward on his own journey toward learning and understanding what the situation is trying to teach him. Now the individual feels strong enough to begin to envision a way of helping himself that reflects strength and creativity (and that is inspired by his **Higher Self**).

Standing by *the person (by expressing caring and compassion) as he navigates his issue gives the* **STRONG message** *that he already has access to all of the strength and Divine wisdom he needs.*

Standing in the way *(by trying to solve the issue) gives a* **strong message**, *too . . . and that message tells him that he needs someone else to fix things for him.*

It is not easy to remember the best way to offer help and support to someone in pain or distress. We tend to feel the very human impulse to make things better for someone we care about.

But the very best way we can help is to offer our listening and caring and compassion and to show by our intention and actions that we know the person can find all of the wisdom he needs within his own heart.

© itmuryn

Kotodama

*The Japanese believe there is a **mystical force inherent in language** . . . that words have a special spiritual effect on the world. They call this concept **Kotodama.***

I love this concept because I am a lover of language, a wordsmith. The words I choose to use are very important to me because I sense and feel their power.

In his book *The Four Agreements* **Don Miguel Ruiz** discusses what he calls *The Impeccability of the Word*. Put very simply, this means using your *Word* in the direction of ***love and truth***. It is so important to be ***authentic*** in our messages. This is the most efficient and direct path to clear communication.

To do this takes courage, a strong sense of self and the motivation and commitment to speak our truth. This is not always easy for sometimes we want to hide from transparency and avoid revealing our thoughts. But those hidden thoughts do not stay undercover forever and will sneak out at a future time in a show of attitude or a statement possibly expressed in an unpleasant moment of tension or stress. Much better to give a mindful, forthright message when we have taken the time and consideration to choose our words with loving and conscious intent.

One important question to ask ourselves is how can I speak my truth AND be sure to express it in a way that would enhance someone's life. This is where the aspect of **LOVE** enters in. And here we can be of great assistance to each other.

If we experience anxiety about the word or words being used in a message, we can take steps to address this situation. By sharing the story of what a particular word or phrase means to us we can help someone understand what message is being received. This may not be the message that is being sent but if a particular word or phrase evokes for us a sense of unease and, if we have not yet been able to fully deal with this issue, the sharing of this context can help increase the caring and compassion transpiring between the two individuals.

The sender of the message can also explain the intention behind the words and, thereby, clarify its meaning from that point of view. Together, the sender and receiver can reach an understanding as to how to best "voice" the message.

In this way, the current soul meaning of the "language" for both individuals can be understood and honored, a true gesture of love.

This kind of communication takes a special intent and effort on the part of both persons involved in the interaction but it has great power to accomplish two things:

To give a clear, authentic and meaningful message

and

To enhance the relationship between two individuals by honoring their souls' points of evolution.

*If we choose to embrace the practice of **Kotodama** as we interact with each other, we will most assuredly strengthen our relationships and, on a global level, we will all move forward into a more loving Universe.*

© Olesia Lishaeva

I Hear Your Heart

*O*ur ears can hear the words that a person speaks *and also the* **inflection** *and* **nuance** *present in those words* **but there is something even more important for us to listen to** *and that something is* **the message of his heart**.

This very special treasure is something we come to know over time and through experience and, sometimes, it is something we can sense about someone. We are able to witness and perceive the glory of a person's heart when he is centered, peaceful, in his power. But this is not always what is happening.

Sometimes the challenges and trials of earth school feel so great for someone that he reacts from his stress, fatigue, or frustration and, sometimes, from his unhealed pain. And his reaction in this moment could easily feel as if it is directed at you.

The message is really for his personal emotional space where he is attempting to navigate his reaction to a painful trigger.

The words he has blurted out are his first attempt to express his distress. The release has not yet taken the path of *Higher Self* and *spiritual evolution*. It is stuck on the first rung of (very human) expression. And it may seem aimed at the closest available object and, in this case, that object may be you.

This moment is such a blessed and holy opportunity to offer love and support to the person who is confronting an old trigger or pain or who is worn down by the stress he is experiencing in his life. We can do so much good at this moment by **NOT** listening to the words of release that appear to stumble out in our direction but by *LISTENING INSTEAD TO THE PERSON'S HEART* which we have already come to sense and know.

As evidenced in his voice, inflection, and words, the openness of his heart has been temporarily blocked by the emotion of hurt or pain but we can choose love to help us access it while he undergoes what is essentially the first stages of self-confrontation. And by choosing *LOVE* we help set the stage for the work he has to do with the issue that has come up for his awareness, acceptance, and release. By affirming that WE KNOW what resides in his heart, we help him access that awareness himself, a step he must take to deal with the issue.

This is a unique opportunity waiting to be recognized.

What a beautiful gift we can give to this individual . . . remembrance and awareness of his *"Best Self"* communicated to him with gentleness and caring and in the moment when he *most needs* to feel that *LOVE!*

A Secret Energy Source

*W*henever we decide to **make a change** in our lives we require a great deal of **ENERGY** and a **free path** for it to flow.

Once we clearly see that the way we are doing things is not working well for us, we are primed and ready for a transformation, but the WAY we try to make that change could be the source of a very big problem. Very often, the first thing we do is **create a picture** of how we can do things differently. This picture usually features a 360-degree turnaround from our usual behavior. We feel motivated and ambitious and so we embark on the journey only to find ourselves stuck in the quicksand of our default.

Here we have envisioned a huge shift in our actions . . . something we really want to do . . . and we get VERY frustrated when it doesn't fall immediately into place. And that starts the verbal barrage we toss at ourselves for not being able to shift things and, even more pointedly, for having practiced such poor behavior and made such bad decisions in the first place.

And herein lies the biggest issue we are now facing. ***We have***

become our self-appointed prosecutor, judge, and jury and are now reciting to ourselves a harangue filled with disappointment and recrimination.

And it's a BIG energy drain. HUGE. And it's seeping the life force out of us.

The fact is that change of any kind is very daunting and uncomfortable. And yet we are beating ourselves up for not being able to kick habits of long standing . . . possibly years of long standing . . . OVERNIGHT! So WHY do we persist in putting ourselves through this agony?

Susan Menanno, a leader of Shamanic Journey Workshops, would say our mind wants to give our spirit indigestion by condemning our perceived inadequacy. *The mind wants to stay in control while our Spirit is growing into the Light.* So how do we stop this intellectual onslaught? We stop it by accessing the heart. We stop it by loving ourselves. We stop JUDGING ourselves because the very act of judgment is LEAKING OUR ENERGY. The more we criticize ourselves, the more we lose this vital life source.

Instead of voicing criticism and condemnation, **Mennano** tells us to:

Call forth in our internal dialog what we want and need.

Voice a clear and sincere intention regarding what we hope to accomplish.

And then trust that we will be gifted with the insight, encouragement, and opportunities to make this happen.

It is then, I believe, that the **Divine Universe** guides us to the perfect circumstances to support us in our desire to transform our behavior. This way of thinking lifts our hearts beautifully and moves us seamlessly into the delightful flow of energy with which Spirit fills our lives. Now we feel strangely free and liberated.

The absence of self-judgment keeps us in the beautiful vibration of evolution and transformation. And the faith that we are loved and guided informs and directs our journey. Now the *energy pathway* to our desired life change is clearly **OPEN** and waits only for us to step forward and accept this gift of grace and opportunity.

© natalia9

Dancing in the Rain

STORMS are mysterious things.

They are gray and dark and feel uncomfortable, as if something is off kilter and is trying to right itself. They can make us feel apprehensive or fearful while we are waiting for them to pass. But even though storms can feel threatening to us, they carry *a beautiful message* . . . crackling and sparking, twisting and turning in tumult and turbulence but eventually *finding their way to clarity and ease.*

*And when they do, there is a glorious release on mother earth, the resonant rhythm of **RAIN.***

*So dance, dance in the rain . . . the beautiful shower of GRACE which illuminates your life, inevitably pointing you to the next highest path of your journey. But **dance, dance also in and through the storm** for that storm is your readiness to acknowledge, confront, feel, and release what you have previously placed aside.*

And this process . . . this journey . . . though challenging is BEAUTIFUL and sings your courage to leave the old, familiar, unconscious habits that have shortchanged your joy and brought you suffering and move instead to embrace new paths that will bring you to freedom and peace.

All of LIFE is a dance. *Don't miss ONE BAR of the beautiful music!*

Painting the Picture of Your Life

*T**HE GIFT OF CREATION* is not reserved for artists, composers, designers, authors.

EVERY ONE of us is a creator and we are creating the journey of our life with every step we take, every decision we make, every thought we think, every word we speak, every emotion we feel. *And we are constantly reinventing that journey* . . . turning in new directions, becoming aware of new concepts, discovering new beauty in life, observing our reactions and behavior, and learning from them or staying stuck in old patterns, resisting new information, dwelling on what feels uncomfortable or difficult and, thereby, digging ourselves deeper into depression or desperation.

We are not static beings. We are constantly dipping into thoughts, memories, and emotions to produce the colors of the art which is our life. And there is great reason here for hope and optimism. Every day, every moment, is an opportunity to influence the unfolding of this *objet d'art*.

We have the OPPORTUNITY to choose how we respond to everything that happens.

We can choose to recognize, acknowledge, and experience our feelings.

We can choose to express those feelings authentically . . . to speak our truth in the best way we know how.

We can not only love ourselves enough to honor and own our feelings, we can also love others enough to respect and honor theirs.

We can choose to accept the flow of life and be open to the lessons it is presenting to us.

We can choose to find the GIFT in every moment.

What makes up the artist's palette of your life?

Are you constantly trying new brushes, new colors, new materials and tools?

Do you stand back, or to the side, to get a different view of what you are creating?

Do the sun and moon illuminate your work and make it sparkle?

Every day, every moment, you bring new perspectives, new vision to your work. How will you *paint your picture* today?

© solar_bird

Are You Ready?

*H*ave *you ever tried to DO something or BE someone because someone else wanted you to and it didn't feel comfortable or natural?*

And yet, perhaps, you still attempted to fulfill someone else's expectations, forcing yourself to *ADAPT* or, even worse, *PRETEND* to be something you are not. Did you do this because you didn't want to disappoint someone or because you wanted to make the other person happy or because you didn't believe you had the right . . . in fact, what you considered the *PRIVILEGE* of being yourself? And what was the result of your performance? I'm betting things didn't end well.

And, if so, perhaps that is because we are never truly peaceful about donning a masquerade to "appear" to be something we are not. *We want to come to the PARTY dressed as ourselves and when we do, we feel natural and free.*

It takes courage and faith and trust to always appear exactly as we truly are. And it takes the awareness and acceptance that who we are at any given moment is a beautiful indication of where we are now landing in the evolution of our life

and

it's the EXPRESSION of our journey, including the joys, the challenges, the triumphs, the unhealed hurts.

*And . . . **it's all good.** It's the tracking of our progress at this point in time for us and for everyone else.* It's the way we move through Earth School. There are many side roads to travel, misadventures to recover from AND victories to celebrate. When we reveal our authentic self, we display a picture of a work in progress based on how much "construction" has been underway and how much has been left undone . . . so far.

***It is important to CELEBRATE our humanity and our common journey** and, most especially, to offer **acceptance** and **support** to ourselves and each other for being fearless enough to display who we truly are, thereby providing the most perfect environment for our spiritual evolution.*

Are you ready?

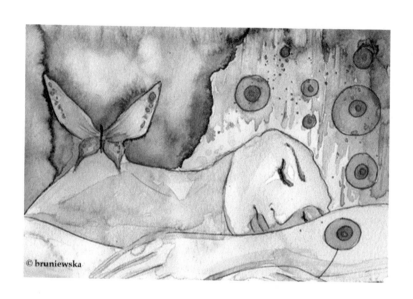

Beautiful Dreamer

*W*inston Churchill described success as the profound desire and strength to move with confidence beyond every impasse we encounter.

What an epic concept! Ardent, passionate, towering, rhapsodic energy that completely sustains itself as we travel in life from one adventure to the next. No matter the quest. Irrespective of the outcome. With no expectations.

ONLY the exuberance of the tinkering and imagining of our intellect.
ONLY the pleasure of our senses dreaming the possibility and then experiencing its manifestation.
ONLY the heart deciding to embrace, decline, or defer what has revealed itself in the process.
ONLY the stray, crucial threads emerging which lead us to our next personally satisfying, cutting edge conception.

ONLY THAT.

After writing this description of the *JOY of the JOURNEY,* I'm ready to don a cape and fly off on yet another adventure for who does not want to play the detective, the dreamer, the magician! The ever fervent seeker of how things mysteriously circle back to us for our pleasure when we have consciously let them roam free to find their connections in the corridors of our heart!

The **SECRET** *to sustaining the life force which always embraces the excitement, the joy, and the turbulence and tumult of the journey*

is

the knowledge that we exist for the purpose of **EXPLORING** ***this magical playground*** *designed to provide us with whatever we can dream.*

> *We are the music makers and we are the*
> *dreamers of dreams.*
>
> *~Arthur O'Shaughnessy*

© kostanproff

Rockin' the Lessons of Earth School

*T*he person who totally embraces life *knows she is the star player in her story and she is enjoying every moment . . . the fun, the lessons, the screw-ups.*

She is very clear that life is ALWAYS teaching her something amazing about herself and she is "all in" for the ride. She feels no pressure to be perfect. (What a relief!) She is just her **real, authentic self** with all of her quirks and idiosyncrasies, unselfconscious about what her actions look like to others.

She is the SOURCE of her own approval.
AND as long as she is open to life's surprises, challenges, and invitations,
AND confident of her ability to embrace and navigate them,
AND is always looking to learn something new, she is good to go.

She does not "phone it in" as the creative arts are fond of saying. She is no watcher from the sidelines. *Oh, no. She is alive and well, jumping and jiving . . . and sometimes kicking* and screaming her way to a new lesson. She wrests the juice out of every moment. She is present, engaged. **She rocks the lessons of earth school.** The jewelry she wears is the stars in HER eyes. She IS the bling. The master who gives herself up to the moment.

She is our inspiration for the life well lived . . . messy, colorful, full of pitfalls and the glorious lessons which accompany them.

THIS starring role is always available in the ongoing performance of earth school just waiting for each and every one of us to step up and step in.

Can you bring it?

Marie Helena

About the Author

*Marie Helena Pokora is an international spiritual blogger whose **Mystic Marks Blog** is read in over one hundred countries. All of the adventures of her life have been preparing her for this moment in time. As a child she was immensely curious and creative and always loved writing. She has a Master's degree in English and has been a college teacher, freelance writer, and a copywriter at an ad agency. Marie has studied spirituality for over twenty years, with special emphasis on energy medicine, Essene Healing, Hakomi, the LifeLine Technique, and past life regression. Now she delights in using her writing skills to share with others the spiritual life lessons she is learning.*

Marie is married and has two daughters. Everyone in her family is a teacher in one of the areas of elementary, secondary, and higher education. Family discussions are always filled with mystical, thought provoking, passionate, and playful interactions.

Marie's blog can be found at
www.mysticmarks.blogspot.com.

Index

Exploring the Present Moment
~Dancing in the Rain
~Fatima's Laughter
~Irish Taxi Drivers

Expressing Compassion
~I Hear Your Heart
~Listen for the Feelings
~Standing By

Fashioning the Philosophy of Your Life
~Are You Ready?
~Dancing in the Rain
~Make Something Beautiful

Returning to Love
~A Secret Energy Source
~I Hear Your Heart
~Kotodama
~Make Something Beautiful
~Setting the Angel Free
~The Eyes and Ears of Love

Surrendering
~Dancing in the Rain
~The Very Special Grace of the Tulip

Afterword

*T*he **Night Blooming Jasmine in Your Heart** *is the first book in the* **Mystic Marks** *series from Dawn Light Press. Upcoming books in this series will explore our luminous journey, the extraordinary gifts available to us from the Divine Universe, and the role Love plays in bringing peace and joy into our lives.*

Please join me in the corridors of the heart for an ongoing celebration of our return to ***Who We Truly Are***!

Marie Helena

CPSIA information can be obtained
at www.ICGtesting.com
Printed in the USA
BVOW05s0124150817
492080BV00021B/66/P